RUMI
IN MANHATTAN

AN EKPHRASTIC COLLECTION OF POETRY AND PHOTOGRAPHY

IMAN TAVASSOLY

Print information available on the last page

Rev. date: 07/09/2018

To order additional copies of this book, contact:
Xlibris
1-888-795-4274
www.Xlibris.com
Orders@Xlibris.com

Uttering a word is like striking a note on the keyboard of the imagination.

(Ludwig Wittgenstein)

For me, photography is a form of meditation. Walking with my camera and framing the expressions of nature and humans, I can focus on the present moment and see how life is created at every single moment. At the same time, poetry is a form of prayer for me which frees my mind by its magical power. My life has been enriched by Rumi's teachings, and since I was eight years old, I have been memorizing his poems, and I have found inspirations in his narrations and stories of human existence and life. In 2012, when I left Iran to come to the USA, the only valuable thing I had in my backpack was Rumi's poetry books of "Masnavi". Rumi was a Persian scholar and mystic who lived in the 13th century. The transformation of his mythical life after meeting with Shams Tabrizi (a mystic and spiritual teacher) and the emergence of a new Rumi which was the prophet of love has always reminded me of the role of rebirth in humans. It is the rebirth which creates new worlds, allows us to reach a new level of understanding and helps us face our existence.

Ekphrasis is a Greek word which means a description. As a term in the art, it is the verbal description of visual arts such as painting or photography. Ekphratic art is the mixture of a picture with words or poetry. In this book, I have used the term ekphrastic art as the integration of photos and poems which are linked together. The ekphrasis of photography here can be considered as poetic photos or a set of pictured poems. The process of linking poems to photos and linking photos to poems is sparked in my mind both before and after capturing the moments with my camera. There are moments when taking a photo inspires me to recite a poem to myself immediately. The photos in this book were taken during my walks in Manhattan, New York between 2012-2018 and the poems are my translation of Rumi's poems which are selected and framed from his works. Some of these poems are small pieces from a larger poem. This reductionist approach was used by Rumi himself in his quatrains which are concise poems. Quatrains are one of the shortest formats in traditional Persian poetry and usually carry an independent notion or story. The Persian version of each poem comes with the English translation, and this has provided a bilingual medium for people interested in Rumi's poems. The goal of this book is not introducing Rumi or his teachings. In fact, the purpose of this ekphrastic collection is to share my moments of merging poetry and photography. The development of this book was an ethereal path for me from photography to poetry via diving in the ocean of Rumi's words. I thank Elnaz Farbod, David Duckett, Sarah Greene, David Meretzky and Melissa Kitson for their help during the preparation of this book.

Iman Tavassoly

پس زبان محرمی خود دیگر است

هم دلی از هم زبانی بهتر است

The language of communion is something else.
Harmonic hearts surpass those tongues speaking the same language.

عاشق به جهان چه غصَه دارد
تا جام شراب وصل برجاست

Not a sorrow does a lover have in this world
for the wine cup of unity never empties.

نقش‌های صنعت دست توییم
پروریده نعمت و نان توییم
چون کبوترزاده برج توییم
در سفر طواف ایوان توییم

Beloved!
We, the lovers,
are signatures by your hands.
Grown by your riches and bread,
we are like pigeons born in your tower.
We are en route flying round your terrace.

مابیم قدیم عشق باره
باقی دگران همه نظاره
چون چرخ حریف آفتابیم
پنهان نشویم چون ستاره

We,
for ages,
in love.
All others are bystanders only.
Like the sky,
we are companions of the sun.
Stars hide from the sun.
We do not.

تا بود که از دیدگان هفت رنگ
دیده‌ای پیدا کند صبر و درنگ
رنگها بینی به جز این رنگ‌ها
گوهران بینی به جای سنگ‌ها

Usual eyes see usual colors.
Eyes with patience can see deeper.
They see gems, not stones.

خندید فرح تا بزنی انگشتک
گردید قدح تا بزنی انگشتک
بنمودت ابروی خود از زیرِ نقاب
چون قوس قزح تا بزنی انگشتک

The bliss smiles at you to dance.
A wine cup is ready for you to dance.
Her eyebrows are unveiled like a rainbow for you to dance.

من هم رباب عشقم و عشقم ربابی است
و آن لطف‌های زخمه رحمانم آرزوست
باقی این غزل را ای مطرب ظریف
زین سان همی شمار که زین سانم آرزوست

I am a psaltery in love's hand.
The notes played are my love.
I long for the melody played by the merciful beloved.
Artful musician!
Play this love song as it is.
It is my dream.

تو در جهان غریبی غربت چه می کنی
قصد کدام خسته جگر می کنی مکن
ای برتر از وجود و عدم بارگاه تو
از خطه وجود گذر می کنی مکن

You are a stranger in this world
How can you live with this loneliness?
To whom do you devote yourself?
Another lover with a wounded heart?
Stay!
You are beyond existence,
nonexistence is your palace.
You cross the land of existence.
Stop!

گر شمس فروشد به غروب او نه فنا شد
از برج دگر آن مه انوار برآمد
گفتار رها کن بنگر آینه عین
کان شبهه و اشکال ز گفتار برآمد

The sun never dies despite sunset,
it rises again, shining in another site of the sky.
Abandon words!
Contemplate the mirror of spirit!
All confusions are from words.

آن بهاران مضمر است اندر خزان
در بهار است آن خزان مگریز از آن

Escape not from autumn.
Autumn is embraced by springtime.

چیست اندر خم که اندر نهر نیست
چیست اندر خانه که اندر شهر نیست
این جهان خمست و دل چون جوی آب
این جهان حجره است و دل شهر عجاب

You find water in a jar, but you can find much in a river.
You find things in a house, but you can find more in the city.
This world: A jar.
The heart: A river.
This world: A house.
The heart: The city of wonders.

مهرِ تو جان نهان بود مهرِ تو بی‌نشان بود
در دل من ز بهرِ تو نقش و نشان چرا چرا

My love for you is concealed.
No need for an address for you in my heart.
No map.

نگفتمت که چو مرغان به سوی دام مرو
بیا که قدرت پرواز و پر و پات منم

"Step not in the trap like other birds!
Come to me instead.
I am the power of your wings to fly."
Didn't I say this to you?

در زمستانشان اگر محبوس کرد
آن غرابان را خدا طاووس کرد

Winter.
Trees are captives,
unsightly like crows.
Springtime.
The almighty frees them,
sightly like peacocks.

در زمستانشان اگر چه داد مرگ
زنده‌شان کرد از بهار و داد برگ

Winter.
Trees are dead.
Springtime,
The almighty resurrects them,
bestows leaves upon them.

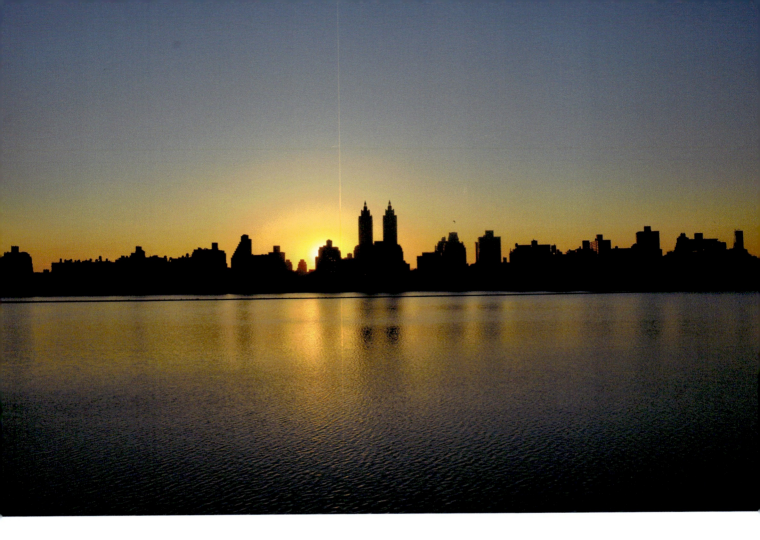

هر جا که هستی حاضری از دور در ما ناظری
شب خانه روشن می شود چون یاد نامت می کنم

You are present every where.
From far away,
you contemplate us.
My home becomes alight,
when your name comes to my mind.

هر کسی اندازهٔ روشن دلی
غیب را بیند به قدر صیقلی
هر که صیقل بیش کرد او بیش دید
بیشتر آمد بر او صورت پدید

The more you polish your heart,
the more light enters,
the more you see the hidden universe.
The more you carve,
the closer you are to the figure.

کوچک بودن بزرگ را کوچک نیست
هم کودکی از کمال خیزد شک نیست

To be little is not a disgrace for a great man.
No doubt,
to be a child comes from mental perfection.

هر کجا دردی دوا آنجا رود
هر کجا فقری نوا آنجا رود
آب کم جو تشنگی آور بدست
تا بجوشد آبت از بالا و پست

Cure follows pain.
Wealth follows poverty.
Look not for water!
Be thirsty!
The water will embrace you.

امروز یکی گردش مستانه کنم
و از کاسه سر ساغر و پیمانه کنم
امروز در این شهر همی گردم مست
می‌جویم عاقلی که دیوانه کنم

Today.
I am drunk,
touring the city.
My head: A wine cup.
I seek a wise man to make him crazed.

آسمانهاست در ولایت جان، کارفرمای آسمان جهان

Set over the soul's realm,
are many heavens.
They govern the sky of this world.

کی باشد آن زمانی گوید مرا فلانی
کای بی‌خبر فنا شو، ای باخبر به رقص آ

I wait to hear a voice calling me:
You, the astray.
Die!
You, the awakened.
Dance!

بیرون ز جهان کفر و ایمان جایی است
کانجا نه مقام هر تر و رعنائی است
جان باید داد و دل به شکرانه جان
آن را که تمنای چنین مأوایی است

Beyond the world of faith and blasphemy,
there is a land forbidden for the fragile.
Visa is granted to those giving away their soul and heart.

گفتم که در انبوهی شهرم که بیابد
آن کس که در انبوهی اسرار مرا یافت

"She will not find me in the city crowd.",
but I am hidden in vain.
She discovered me in the crowd of secrets.

بیرون ز جهان و جان یکی دایه ماست
دانستن او نه در خور پایه ماست
در معرفتش همین قدر دانم
ما سایه اوئیم و جهان سایه ماست

Further than the universe,
beyond the soul,
there is a presence keeping an eye on us,
and the only thing I know:
"We are her shadow and the universe is our shadow."

....که ز هر دل تا دل آمد روزنه

There is a window through which two hearts gaze at each other.

قلم بگرفته نقاشان که جانم مست کف‌هاشان
که تصویرات زیباشان جمال شاخسار آمد

Painters,
in their hands brushes.
My soul,
drunk of art of their hands.
They create graceful images reflected in the beauty of trees.

در جان تو جانی است بجو آن جان را
در کوه تو کانی است بجو آن کان را
صوفی رونده گر توانی می‌جوی
بیرون تو مجوز خود بجو تو آن را

There is love in your soul.
Seek that love!
Your body: A mountain, a gem buried in it.
Seek that gem!
You are a seeker en route.
Seek!
Seek not outside yourself,
Seek within!

راهی ز زبان ما به دل پیوسته است
که اسرار جهان و جانِ در او پیوسته است
تا هست زبان بسته گشاده است آن راه
چون گشت زبان گشاده آن ره بسته است

From tongue to heart:
A Path.
Carved on it,
the secrets of the universe and the soul.
Your mouth closes,
the path opens.
Silence!
Words close this path.

اندیشه مکن بکن تو خود را در خواب
که اندیشه ز روی مه حجاب است حجاب
دل چون ماه است در دل اندیشه مدار
انداز تو اندیشه گری را در آب

The mind.
Do not follow it!
Detach from it, as when you sleep.
The heart is a shining moon.
The mind is a cloud.
It weakens that light.
Banish your mind!
Cast it in water!

خویش را عریان کن از فضل و فضول
تا کند رحمت به تو هر دم نزول

No knowledge.
No thought of perfection.
Drops of grace upon you at every moment.

ره آسمان درون است پر عشق را بجنبان
پر عشق چون قوی شد غم نردبان نماند

The path to the sky passes through your heart.
Flap the wings of love!
Worry not!
You need no ladder to ascend.
Earn mighty wings of love!

خاموش که خاموشی بهتر ز عسل نوشی
درسوز عبارت را بگذار اشارت را

Silence!
Silence is better.
Burn the words!
Abandon the remarks!

یک دست جام باده و یک دست جعد یار
رقصی چنین میانه میدانم آرزوست

A cup of wine in hand.
Running my fingers through her hair.
I long for such a dance amid the city square.

آن را که مدد از اندرون است
ز این عالم بی‌مدد نترسد

Those empowered within,
have no fear of this unhelpful world.

پنهان ز دیده‌ها و همه دیده‌ها از اوست

آن آشکار صنعت پنهانم آرزو است

The one who created all eyes is hidden from all.
Her art,
everywhere.
Her face,
veiled.
I long for her.

اى ديده من جمال خود اندر جمال تو
آيينه گشتهام همه بهرِ خيال تو

In your grace, I have seen mine.
You, the light.
I, the mirror.

کف دریاست صورت‌های عالم

ز کف بگذر اگر اهل صفایی

All images in the world are the ocean's foam.
To be of joyous people, go beyond the foams,
Dive!

اندر بهار وحی خدا درس عام گفت
بنوشت باغ و مرغ به تکرار می‌رود

Springtime:
The first lesson,
a revelation.
Notes from the garden.
A bird repeats.

گفت تماشای جهان عکس ماست
هم برِ ما باش که با ما خوش است

"To see me,
Contemplate the universe!",
she said.
"Stay with me! This contemplation is joyous with me."

راه هموارست و زیرش دام ها
قحط معنی در میان   نام ها

The path seems level,
but traps are underneath.
So many glorious names,
but no genuineness.

ز اول که حدیث عاشقی بشنودم
جان و دل و دیده در رهش فرسودم
گفتم که مگر عاشق و معشوق دواند
خود هر دو یکی بود من احول بودم

I heard the tale of love.
With eyes on the path of love,
I weary my soul and my heart.
My eyes were cocked,
I thought the lover and beloved were two,
but they were one.

تو آسمان منی من زمین به حیرانی
که دم به دم ز دل من چه چیز رویانی

You are the sky.
I am the wandering Earth.
At every moment,
you grow something in my heart.

یکی جانیم در اجسام   مفرق
اگر خردیم اگر پیریم و برنا

We,
child,
young,
old,
many bodies,
one soul.

چو ما در چنگ عشق اندر فتادیم
چه کم آید بر ما چنگ و سرنا
رباب و چنگ عالم گر بسوزد
بسی چنگی پنهانی است یارا

Love seized us.
Harp and horn make no joy anymore.
If all harps and psalteries in the world burn,
worry not!
Many hidden players are there.
They play for us.

این سو جهان، آن سو جهان، بنشسته من بر آستان

A world here.
A world there.
Me,
between.

در کف ندارم سنگ من، با کس ندارم جنگ من
با کس نگیرم تنگ من، زیرا خوشم چون گلستان

I carry no stone in my hands,
I fight with no one,
I upset no one,
for I am like a bloomed garden.

اوست نشسته در نظر، من به کجا نظر کنم
اوست گرفته شهر دل، من به کجا سفر برم

The beloved is everywhere.
Turning my eyes,
 I only see her.
The beloved seized the city of my heart.
Where else is there for me to travel?

سایه‌ای و عاشقی بر آفتاب
شمس آید سایه لاگردد شتاب

You are a shadow,
in love with The Sun.
Yet when The Sun arrives,
you die.

در این دم، همدمی آمد خمش کن
که او ناگفته می داند خمش کن

This moment,
A companion arrives.
Not even a whisper!
She knows all words before you utter them.
Silence!

هر اندیشه که در دل دفن کردی
یکایک بر تو بر خواند خمش کن

You bury thoughts in your heart,
one by one.
The beloved will read them to you,
one by one.
Silence!

نظر در نامه می‌دارد ولی با لب نمی‌خواند
همی داند کز این حامل چه صورت زایدش فردا

The beloved sees your letter.
She reads in silence.
Words are pregnant with meaning.
She knows what will be born tomorrow.

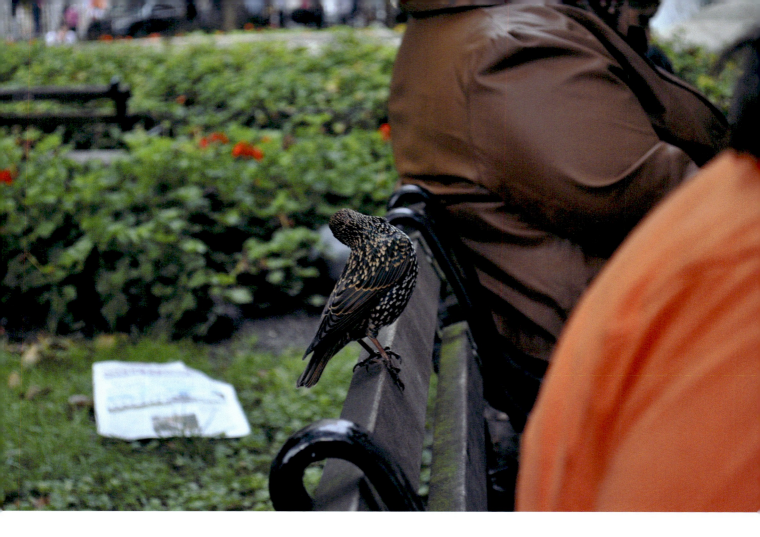

چه گوهری تو که کس را به کف بهای تو نیست
جهان چه دارد در کف که آن عطای تو نیست
مبارک است هوای تو بر همه مرغان
چه نامبارک مرغی که در هوای تو نیست

You are a priceless gem.
Everything existing in the world is bestowed by you.
Desire for you is like the air for birds,
they are blessed flying in it.
The bird with no desire for you is cursed.

فقیر و عارف و درویش وانگهی هشیار
مجاز بود چنین نام‌ها تو پنداری

Mindful,
poor,
mystic,
dervish,
are all fake names.

در این خاک در این خاک در این مزرعه پاک
به جز مهر به جز عشق دگر تخم نکاریم

The human soul is a blessed farmland.
When it comes to dust,
let us plant nothing except love and grace.

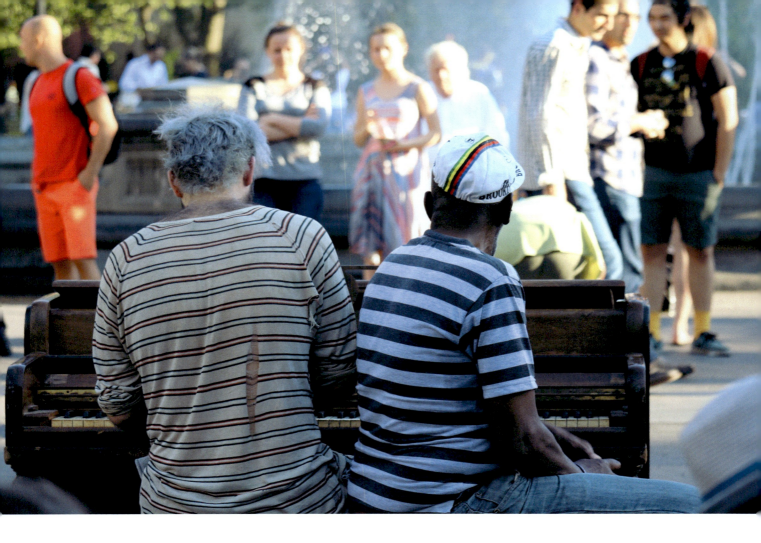

صلا زدند همه عاشقان طالب را
روان شوید به میدان پی تماشا را
دلی که پند نگیرد ز هیچ دلداری
بر او گمار دمی آن شراب گیرا را

A calling for all seekers in love:
"Go to the city square to watch!"
There are hearts that welcome no advice from any beloved,
let the red wine guard them.

برخیز بخیلانه در خانه فروبند
که آنجا که تویی خانه شود گلشن و صحرا

Up! Close the doors! Let no one in!
A house filled only with you becomes a garden

هر خوشی که فوت شد از تو مباش اندوهگین
کو به نقشی دیگر آید سوی تو می دان یقین

Worry not!
All joys you lost on the path,
will return in another form.
No doubt!

همه فانی و خوان وحدت تو
مدام است و مدام است و مدام است
چو چشم خود بمالم خود به جز تو
کدام است و کدام است و کدام است

Everything is mortal.
Your unity feast is immortal.
Immortal.
Immortal.
Rubbing my eyes,
awakened,
there is nothing but you.
You.
You.

اگر یک روز باقی باشد از دی
زمین لب بسته است و گل نهفته است

Earth,
silent.
Still winter,
even if the last day:
Blossoms are hidden.

Printed in the United States
By Bookmasters